I0821232

★★★★★
MLB TEAMS

Tampa Bay RAYS

KENNY ABDO

Fly!
An Imprint of Abdo Zoom
abdobooks.com

abdobooks.com

Published by Abdo Zoom, a division of ABDO, P.O. Box 398166, Minneapolis, Minnesota 55439.

Printed in the United States of America, North Mankato, Minnesota.
102025
012026

Photo Credits: Alamy, AP Images, Getty Images, Shutterstock
Production Contributors: Kenny Abdo, Jennie Forsberg, Grace Hansen
Design Contributors: Candice Keimig, Neil Klinepier

Library of Congress Control Number: 2025936813

Publisher's Cataloging-in-Publication Data

Names: Abdo, Kenny, author.
Title: Tampa Bay Rays / by Kenny Abdo
Description: Minneapolis, Minnesota : Abdo Zoom, 2026 | Series: MLB teams | Includes online resources and index.
Identifiers: ISBN 9798384940340 (lib. bdg.) | ISBN 9798384941101 (ebook) | ISBN 9798384941484 (read-to-me ebook)
Subjects: LCSH: Tampa Bay Rays (Baseball team)--Juvenile literature. | Baseball teams--Juvenile literature. | Professional sports--Juvenile literature. | Sports franchises--Juvenile literature. | Major League Baseball (Organization)--Juvenile literature.
Classification: DDC 796.357--dc23

Table of CONTENTS

Rays 4

Batter Up! 8

Grand Slams 14

Hall of Fame 24

Glossary 30

Online Resources 31

Index 32

RAYS

Riding the Tampa Bay tide with speed and skill, the Rays make a splash in every game and dare any rival to risk getting stung!

With waves of big wins, star players, and **record**-setting moments, the Rays have built a history that keeps Tampa Bay fans hooked!

RAYS

BATTER UP!

The Tampa Bay Devil Rays began play in Florida in 1998 as one of Major League Baseball's newest teams. The early seasons were tough. In its first year, the team finished last in the **division** with a 63-99 **record**. There were many challenges still to come.

MCGRIFF

In 2008, the team dropped *Devil* to become the Tampa Bay Rays. The team also changed its uniform design and colors. The original logo of a devil ray was replaced by a sunburst. That year, the Rays finished 97–65 and made their first World Series. Though they lost to the Phillies, the young Rays were finally competitors.

In 2010, the Rays won the **AL** East. Breakout pitcher David Price finished with a 19-6 **record**, a 2.72 **ERA**, and 188 strikeouts. The Rays would lose to their first playoff opponent, the Rangers, in five games.

TB
RAYS

GRAND SLAMS

The Rays kept the pressure on and made the playoffs in 2011 and 2013. James Shields threw heat through the 2012 season, while Ben Zobrist earned **All-Star** status in 2013. The Rays made more playoff runs in the years that followed. In 2019, the team had one of the best seasons in team history with a 96-66 **record**!

Globe Life Field
WORLD SERIES
LAST PLAY
89 MPH
AROZARENA
56
POWERADE
Extreme networks
CHEVROLET
SERIES

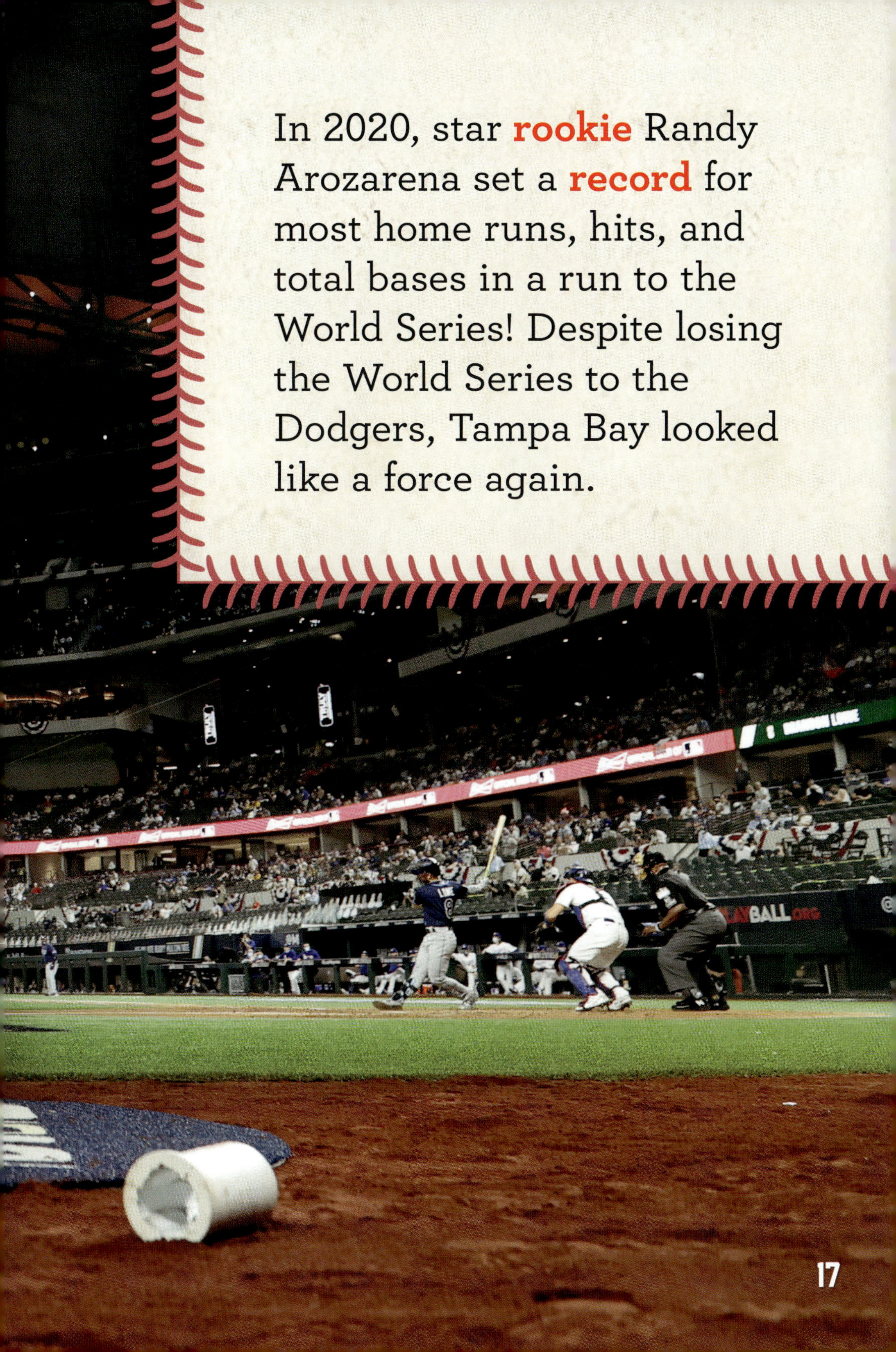

In 2020, star **rookie** Randy Arozarena set a **record** for most home runs, hits, and total bases in a run to the World Series! Despite losing the World Series to the Dodgers, Tampa Bay looked like a force again.

RAYS
TB

The Rays stayed hot during the 2021 season, winning 100 games for the first time and taking the **AL** East. Brandon Lowe had a career-best offensive year, hitting .247 with 39 home runs, 99 **RBIs**, and 97 runs scored in 149 games.

Keeping the pressure on in 2022, the Rays finished 86–76 and made the playoffs. In 2023, the team won 99 games and earned second place in the **AL** East. Star pitcher Shane McClanahan struck out 194 batters in 2022 and 121 in 2023.

TB
RAYS

The Rays had a tough 2024 season, finishing 80–82. The season highlight came from Lowe. The second baseman hit a **walk-off** three-run homer to beat the Cubs 5–2 at Tropicana Field.

The Rays followed up with another losing season in 2025. A number of key players were out with injuries. However, Rays fans hoped that the young core of players could finally lead the team to its first World Series title.

HALL OF FAME

Evan Longoria is the Rays' all-time leader in home runs, **RBIs**, **doubles**, and games played. He won **Rookie** of the Year in 2008 and helped lead the team to its first World Series appearance.

In the 2008 playoffs, Longoria hit two homers in his first two at-bats. In 2011, he smashed a **walk-off** homer to clinch a playoff spot. He joined the Rays Hall of Fame in 2026.

Fred McGriff brought power and experience to the Rays in the team's early years. He became an **All-Star** and hit 99 home runs during his time in Tampa Bay. McGriff also drove in 359 runs and helped give the new team a strong start. His big bat and leadership helped put the Rays on the map.

FREDERICK STANLEY MCGRIFF
"FRED" "CRIME DOG"
TORONTO, A.L. 1986-90; SAN DIEGO, N.L. 1991-93;
ATLANTA, N.L. 1993-97; TAMPA BAY, A.L. 1998-2001, 2004;
CHICAGO, N.L. 2001-02; LOS ANGELES, N.L. 2003
CRUSHED THE BALL WITH CONSISTENCY FOR 19 SEASONS, USING SMOOTH LEFT-HANDED SWING TO AMASS 493 HOME RUNS AND 1,550 RBI. HIT 30-OR-MORE HOMERS 10 TIMES, THE FIRST TO DO SO FOR FIVE DIFFERENT TEAMS. FINISHED AMONG HIS LEAGUE'S TOP FIVE IN LONG BALLS AND OPS IN SEVEN STRAIGHT SEASONS, 1988-94, TOPPING THE A.L. IN HOMERS IN 1989 AND THE N.L. IN 1992. DELIVERED HEROICS AS CLEANUP HITTER FOR 1995 WORLD SERIES CHAMPION BRAVES AND HIT .303 IN 50 CAREER POSTSEASON GAMES. THREE-TIME SILVER SLUGGER AT FIRST BASE AND FIVE-TIME ALL-STAR EARNED 1994 ALL-STAR GAME MVP HONORS.

RAYS

David Price was one of the Rays' best pitchers. He won the **Cy Young Award** in 2012 after leading the league with 20 wins. Price was a five-time **All-Star** in his career.

GLOSSARY

All-Star – an athlete named to the yearly baseball contest where top players from the AL and the NL compete against each other.

American League (AL) – one of two 15-team leagues that make up MLB.

Cy Young Award – an annual American baseball award given to the best pitcher in each of the two MLB leagues.

division – a number of teams grouped together in a sport for competitive purposes.

double – a type of hit where the batter safely reaches second base on a single play.

Earned-Run Average (ERA) – the average number of earned runs per game scored against a pitcher.

record – the top achievement by a team or player that no one has done before; the total number of wins and losses a team has in a season.

rookie – a professional athlete in his or her first season in a sport.

Runs Batted In (RBI) – a statistic that credits a batter for making a play that allows a run to be scored.

walk-off – any victory in which the home team scores the winning run in the bottom of the final inning.

ONLINE RESOURCES

To learn more about the Tampa Bay Rays, please visit **abdobooklinks.com** or scan this QR code. These links are routinely monitored and updated to provide the most current information available.

INDEX

Arozarena, Randy 17

awards 29

Cubs (team) 22

Dodgers (team) 17

Longoria, Evan 24, 25

Lowe, Brandon 19, 22

McClanahan, Shane 20

McGriff, Fred 26

Phillies (team) 10

Price, David 12, 29

Rangers (team) 12

Shields, James 14

Zobrist, Ben 14